This book belongs to…

_____

_____

FREE Monthly Stories & Dances Workshop

JOIN our Facebook Group "Raise Multicultural Kids" for details

www.CultureGroove.com/Free

Pronunciation Guide

Bua – Boo-aaa

Dahi Handi – Duh-hee Haan-dee

Janambhoomi – Jun-muh-bhoo-mee

Janmashtami – Jun-mah-sh-tummy

Kolam – Koh-lum

Kumil – Koo-mill

Mathura – Muh-thoo-raa

Radha – Raa-dhaa

Raslila – Raas-leela

Note for parents: Our books provide a glimpse into the beautiful cultural diversity of India, including occasional mythology references. Given India's size and diversity, Krishna Janmashtami (birthday) is celebrated in a multitude of different ways. In this book, we showcase elements of Janmashtami that are best suited for young readers to follow.

Copyright © 2016, 2017, 2018, 2019 by Bollywood Groove™, Culture Groove. All rights reserved. This book or any portion thereof may not be reproduced or used in any manner whatsoever without the express written permission of the publisher except for the use of brief quotations in a book review.
Printed in the United States of America. First Edition.

Maya & Neel's India Adventure Series, Book 12

Let's Celebrate Krishna's Birthday!

Culture Groove
Raise Multicultural Kids
Connect Kids to their Roots

Written by:
Ajanta & Vivek

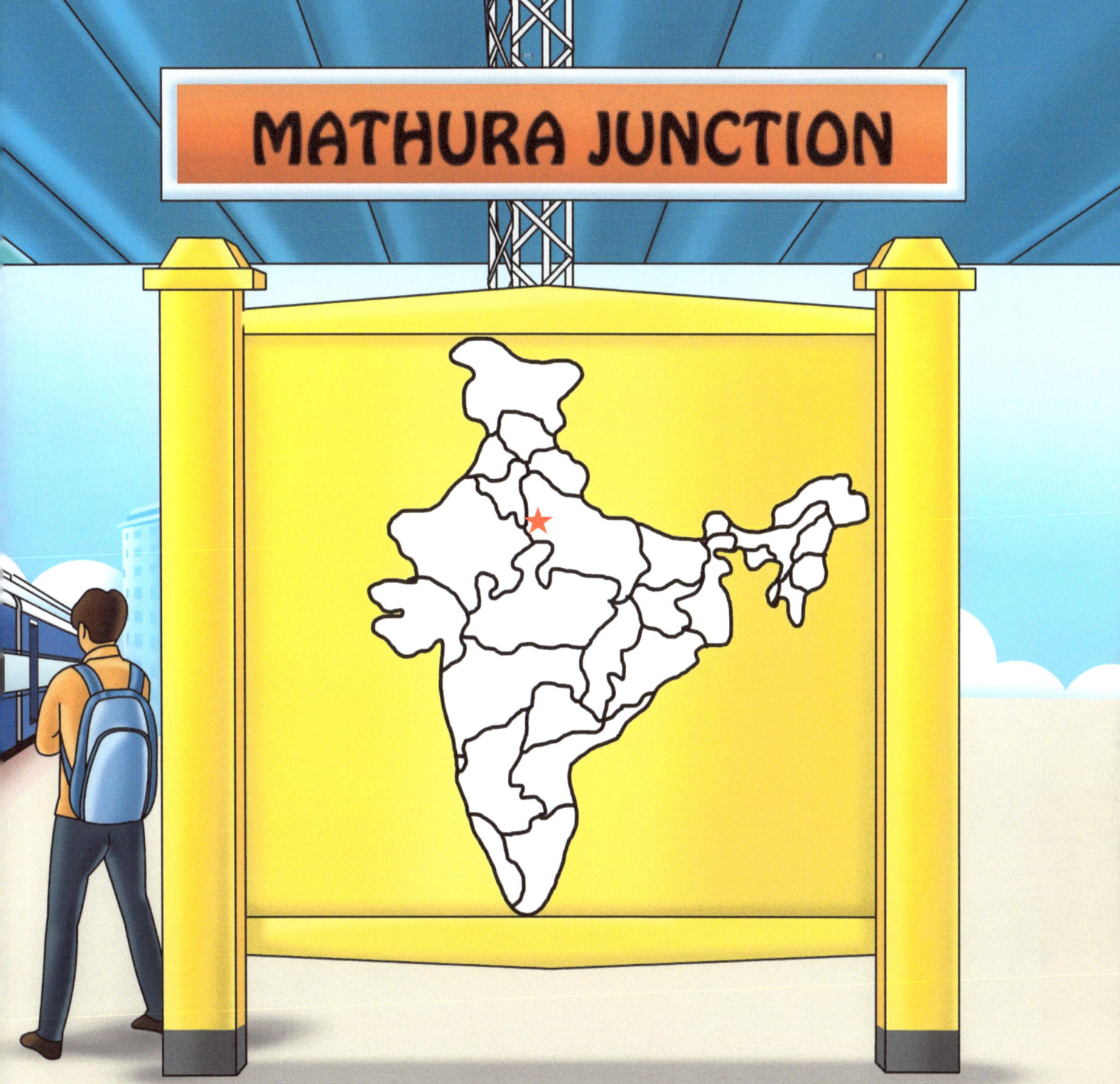

This is a map of India. India is a big country. It has many states, languages, festivals, and dances.

Do you see the red star on the map? That is Mathura, where Krishna was born.

People in Mathura celebrate Krishna's birthday with a big festival called *Janmashtami*.

Maya, Neel and Chintu arrive at their Auntie Leela's house.

Leela Auntie is Maya & Neel's dad's sister. In Hindi, dad's sister is called *Bua*.

Leela Auntie rushes to give them a hug. "Welcome kids," she says "I am so happy that you could make it to Mathura."

"Leela *Bua*, what should we do while we are here?" Maya asks.

"A really fun festival called *Janmashtami* starts tomorrow. *Janmashtami* is Krishna's birthday celebration" *Bua* explains.

"Who is Krishna, *Bua*?" Neel asks. "Oh, let me tell you all about him," *Bua* says excitedly.

INFO ZOOM — Who is Krishna?

Some people in India pray to Krishna as a God. Krishna plays the flute. He wears a peacock feather on his head. And he looooves butter!

Stories say, a mean king had locked Krishna's mom and dad in a room. Krishna's mom and dad knew that when Krishna would be born, the evil king would take him away.

Krishna was born at midnight. Suddenly, the guards outside the room magically fell asleep. Krishna's dad put him in a basket. The room's doors opened up and Krishna's dad walked out with the basket on his head.

Krishna's dad had to take him far away to keep him safe. On his way, he had to cross a river. It started to rain very hard.

Suddenly, a snake with many heads showed up. The snake covered the basket like an umbrella so that Krishna would not get wet in the rain.

Krishna's birthday is celebrated at midnight. His birthday festival is called *Janmashtami*.

"Maya, Neel, Chintu, try out your *Janmashtami* clothes!" *Bua* says as she gives them some fun and colorful outfits. The kids put on their clothes with big smiles.

"I look like Krishna!" Neel exclaims. "Who do I look like?" Maya wonders. "You will find out soon," *Bua* says with a mysterious smile.

Neel loves his new flute. Maya walks around with some cool clay pots.

"Can you kids stay up till midnight? We will have our own celebration then," *Bua* says with a big smile.

Maya, Neel and Chintu instantly nod their heads.

"We can't wait!" they exclaim in unison.

Right at midnight, *Bua* shows them her two little statues.

"The one with the flute is Krishna but who is the other one?" Neel asks. "Radha. She is Krishna's best friend." *Bua* explains. "Aha, so I am dressed like Radha," Maya exclaims.

"First, we give them a bath" *Bua* says as she pours milk on the statues. Then she puts beautiful little outfits on them.

Next, she places them in a cradle and gently swings them. Maya and Neel stare in wonder.

Then, *Bua* gives the kids plates of sweets and fruits. Maya, Neel and Chintu finish off every bit of the yummy food.

The kids wander over to the window. "Whoa, what is that building outside?" Neel asks.

"That is the *Janmabhoomi* temple.

Stories say that the temple is built exactly where Krishna was born. They are also having a midnight birthday celebration for Krishna," *Bua* explains.

Maya and Neel look in awe at the thousands of lights. They can hear the sounds of bells and music from the inside.

"I have a surprise for you!" *Bua* says. "Tomorrow, we will go on a mystery trip."

"Where are we going, *Bua*?" Neel asks. "No, no," *Bua* laughs, "it's a surprise."

The next morning, *Bua* and the kids get on a plane. "Kids, we are going to Mumbai!" *Bua* finally shares.

"We've been there before. We love it!" Maya replies.

"This time, you will see how Mumbai celebrates *Janmashtami*. It involves a lot of climbing." *Bua* says with a mysterious smile.

"But while we travel, let me tell you another Krishna story."

STORY TIME: Krishna & Kaliya

Once, a scary snake named Kaliya came to live in the Yamuna river. Because of Kaliya, the people of Mathura were very scared to go near the water.

One day, Krishna and his friends were playing next to the river. While playing, the ball fell in the river.

No one wanted to get the ball because of Kaliya.

Krishna was very brave and he fearlessly jumped in the river. Kaliya attacked him right away but Krishna fought him bravely.

Krishna was so brave that he even climbed on Kaliya's head and started dancing! After some time, the snake got too tired to fight anymore and gave up. Kaliya went away from the river and never came back.

Wasn't Krishna so brave?

They finally reach Mumbai.

They see hundreds of people gathered on the streets.

"This is called *Dahi Handi*. The one who reaches the top and breaks the pot, wins." *Bua* explains.

"Do you know why they do this, kids?" *Bua* asks.

The kids shake their heads.

"It is because Krishna did the same thing. Let me tell you that story," *Bua* says.

STORY TIME

Krishna sneaks butter

Krishna loved butter.

When his mom was not looking, he would sneak in and eat butter straight from the butter pot.

To keep Krishna from sneaking the butter, his mom decided to hang the butter pot high up from the ceiling.

Krishna and his friends tried to get the butter. They jumped up high in the air but could not reach it.

Then, Krishna came up with a clever plan.

Krishna made his friends form a human pyramid and climbed on them.

He went all the way up to the top and reached the butter pot.

Krishna brought it down and they all had a fun, butter eating party!

"Oh look, someone is about to climb the pyramid" Neel shouts.

The pyramid has many people now. A man starts to climb. Everyone claps and cheers. He finally reaches the top.

Chintu is excited. He quickly runs up the pyramid as well. Neel, Maya and *Bua* clap in joy. Chintu helps break the pot! The team wins the *Dahi Handi* competition.

"That was so amazing! *Bua*, do people do anything else on *Janmashtami*?" Maya asks.

"Yes, there are many ways to celebrate. Let me tell you more." *Bua* replies.

INFO ZOOM ## Janmashtami around India

In Manipur, they act out Krishna and Radha stories in musical plays. These plays are called *Raslila*.

The fun outfits that women wear are called *Kumil*.

In Tamil Nadu, they draw beautiful patterns called *Kolam*. They even draw footprints that point inside their house.

The footprints are drawn to welcome Krishna inside their house.

"Wow! That was so much fun. *Janmashtami* is such a beautiful and fun festival!" Neel says.

"I agree. From the midnight celebration to the *Dahi Handi* competition, it was such an exciting adventure" Maya adds.

"We cannot wait for our next adventure. We wonder where that will be. We hope you can join us then," Maya, Neel and Chintu say.

"Until then, Namaste!"

INFO RECAP

Let's look back on our wonderful trip to celebrate Krishna's B'day

What is Janmashtami? *Krishna's birthday celebration*

Who is Krishna's best friend? *Radha*

Where is the Janmabhoomi temple? *Where Krishna was born*

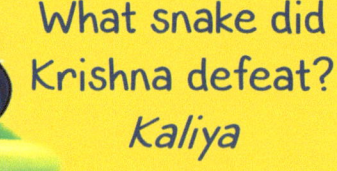 **What snake did Krishna defeat?** *Kaliya*

What is the musical play about Krishna's life called? *Raslila*

What musical instrument does Krishna play? *Flute*

What feather does Krishna have on his head? *Peacock feather*

At what time was Krishna born? *Midnight*

What does Krishna like to eat? *Butter*

What is the cool pattern that they draw on the floor? *Kolam*

What is the competition they see in Mumbai? *Dahi Handi*

About the Authors

Ajanta Chakraborty was born in Bhopal, India, and moved to North America in 2001. She earned an MS in Computer Science from the University of British Columbia and also earned a Senior Diploma in Bharatanatyam, a classical Indian dance, to feed her spirit.

Ajanta quit her corporate consulting job in 2011 and took the plunge to run Bollywood Groove (and also Culture Groove) full-time. The best part of her work day includes grooving with classes of children as they leap and swing and twirl to a Bollywood beat.

Vivek Kumar was born in Mumbai, India, and moved to the US in 1998. Vivek has an MS in Electrical Engineering from The University of Texas, Austin, and an MBA from the Kellogg School of Management, Northwestern University.

Vivek has a very serious day job in management consulting. But he'd love to spend his days leaping and swinging, too.

We have been featured on:

We are independent authors who want to help **Raise Multicultural Kids**! We rely on your support to sustain our work:

- ✓ Drop us an Amazon review at: **CultureGroove.com/books**
- ✓ **Share our books as Gifts & Party Favors** (bulk order discounts)
- ✓ Schedule our unique **'Dancing Bookworms' Virtual Author Visits**
- ✓ Join our **FREE** Monthly Stories & Dances workshops: **CultureGroove.com/FREE**

Many thanks!

Culture Groove
Raise Multicultural Kids

Lightning Source UK Ltd.
Milton Keynes UK
UKHW050821210122
397492UK00002B/35